GRANDPA'S GARDEN
WRITTEN & ILLUSTRATED BY KIM KILB

Grandpa's Garden

© 2023 by Kim Kilb

All rights reserved. No portion of this book may be reproduced, stored in a retrieval system, or transmitted in any form or by any means—electronic, mechanical, photocopy, recording, scanning, or other—except for brief quotations in critical reviews or articles, without the prior written permission of the publisher.

Published in Racine, Wisconsin, by Kim Kilb

Illustrations by Kim Kilb
The illustrations in this book were rendered digitally

Layout and format design by Lauren Hengeveld

ISBN: 979-8-9900375-0-2

Library of Congress Cataloging-in-Publication Data is on file

Printed in the United States of America

Dedicated to
the memory of my beloved grandpa,
Ron Slamka, whose pure love of his
family, joy for life and continued
support of my artistic pursuits
inspired "Grandpa's Garden."
In honor of my grandmas,
Marlene Slamka and Viola Mierow,
both sources of unwavering love.
To my children, husband
and family- your encouragement
cultivated this blossoming journey.

Love you♡

GRANDPA ALWAYS HAD A GREEN
THUMB.
Not a green
thumb

HE GREW BEAUTIFUL FLOWERS,
VIBRANT JUICY VEGETABLES,
PLUMP RED RASPBERRIES...

THEY SPRUNG UP FROM THE SOIL
JUST TO SEE HIS FACE.

HIS GARDEN ALWAYS WAS,
AND SO HE WOULD ALWAYS BE TOO.

dried
chinese
lanterns
for decor

UNTIL ONE DAY HE WASN'T ANYMORE.

FERN LAY ALONE IN GRANDPA'S GARDEN.
TIME MOVED SO SLOWLY SINCE HE LEFT.
HOW COULD THE SUN STILL SHINE WITHOUT
HIM? HOW COULD THE BIRDS SING?
A SALTY TEAR ROLLED DOWN HER CHEEK AS SHE
WATCHED THE LONELY BEES.

"HELLO LITTLE BEES."
THEY FLEW FROM FLOWER TO FLOWER,
BUZZING AND WORKING AWAY.

"HOW DO YOU KEEP WORKING
WITHOUT HIM?" SHE ASKED.

"HE'S NOT GONE," A BEE REPLIED.
"HE'S IN THE BREEZE THAT COOLS OUR
WINGS ON A HOT SUMMER DAY AS WE
WORK TO POLLINATE FLOWERS IN
HIS GARDEN."

THAT SAME BREEZE BLEW
GENTLY THROUGH THE FLOWERS,
RUSTLING THE LEAVES ON THEIR STEMS
AND THE HAIR ON FERN'S FACE.

FERN TURNED AND LOOKED AT
THE FLOWERS. THEY LOOKED THE
SAME AS THEY ALWAYS HAD—
AS BEAUTIFUL AS BEFORE, BUT
WERE THEY? HOW COULD
THEY BE? SHE NOTICED A
PARTICULARLY SMALL BLOSSOM.

"HELLO LITTLE BUD," SHE SAID.
"HOW WILL YOU BLOOM WITHOUT
HIM?"

"HE IS NOT GONE." THE BUD
REPLIED. "HE IS HERE IN THE
SUN THAT WARMS MY PETALS
AND GIVES ME THE ENERGY I
NEED TO BLOSSOM AND
GROW."

Grandpa's pickles

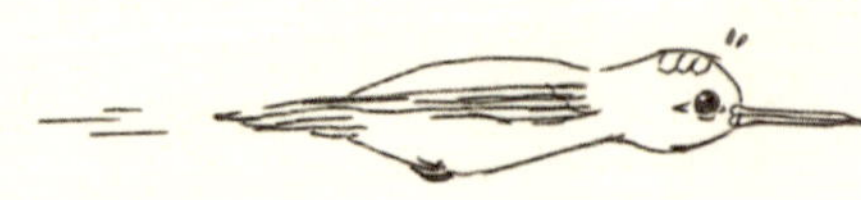

THE SUN SHONE DOWN AND WRAPPED
FERN IN A WARMTH LIKE GRANDPA'S HUG.

AS SHE SAT AMONGST THE FLOWERS,
A SPRIGHTLY HUMMINGBIRD STOPPED
TO SIP SOME NECTAR FROM A HOLLYHOCK
NEARBY. THE SHIMMERING BIRD SEEMED
UNTROUBLED BY THE WORLD.

"HELLO LITTLE BIRD."
THE HUMMINGBIRD TURNED TO FERN-
"HOW WILL YOU KEEP FLYING WITHOUT HIM?" SHE
ASKED.
"HE IS NOT GONE." THE TINY BIRD REPLIED.

"HE IS HERE IN THE FLOWERS THAT BLOOM, IN THE SUN THAT SHINES AND IN THE BREEZE THAT BLOWS. HE IS ALL AROUND AND EVER-WORKING, AND THAT IS WHY I WILL BE EVER-WORKING TOO — SO THAT HIS GARDEN WILL ALWAYS BE.

FERN FELT THE SOFT GRASS
AND SMELLED THE SWEET SOIL.

"IF THE FLOWERS CAN STILL BLOOM,
THE BEES CAN STILL WORK, AND THE
BIRDS CAN STILL FLY...IF MY HEART
CAN STILL BEAT...
HE ISN'T REALLY GONE AFTER
ALL."
rhubarb, for grandma's pie

THE love of gardening IS
A SEED THAT ONCE SEWN NEVER
DIES, BUT ALWAYS GROWS AND
GROWS TO AN ENDURING AND
EVER-INCREASING SOURCE OF
HAPPINESS.
-GERTRUDE JEKYLL

My grandpa grew the most amazing garlic. You won't find his exact variety anywhere. Passing his practices to my sister, its legacy continues on her farm.

ABOUT THE AUTHOR/ILLUSTRATOR:
I'VE ALWAYS LOVED MAKING WHIMSICAL, JOYFUL ART. ALTHOUGH I AM NOT MUCH OF A WRITER, I FOUND INSPIRATION IN THE MIDST OF GRIEF AFTER THE UNEXPECTED LOSS OF MY GRANDPA. I WANTED TO HONOR THE MEMORY OF MY GRANDPA THROUGH A STORY CENTERED AROUND ONE OF HIS GREATEST PASSIONS - GARDENING. THIS BOOK NOT ONLY SERVES AS A PERSONAL RELEASE, BUT ALSO AS A GIFT TO MY GRANDMA AND A TRIBUTE TO THE PROUD LEGACY OF A FAMILY BONDED BY LOVE. I HOPE I CREATED SOMETHING THAT SPEAKS TO BOTH CHILDREN AND ADULTS, THROUGH A WORLD WHERE MEMORIES, EMOTIONS AND VIBRANT ARTWORK INTERTWINE. WITH A CREATIVE SPIRIT FUELED BY A DESIRE TO MAKE SOMETHING THAT TRULY RESONATES, I HOPE TO HAVE CREATED A STORY THAT LEAVES A LASTING MARK ON YOUR HEART.
-KIM KILB